THE OFFICIAL
RANGERS
ANNUAL
2003

Written by
Douglas Russell

g

A Grange Publication

© 2002. Published by Grange Communications Ltd., Edinburgh, under licence from Rangers Football Club. Printed in the EU.

Every effort has been made to ensure the accuracy of information within this publication but the publishers cannot be held responsible for any errors or omissions. Views expressed are those of the author and do not necessarily represent those of the publishers or the football club.
All rights reserved.

With thanks to Rangers photographer, Lynne Cameron

ISBN 1-902704-29-0

CONTENTS

Playing for the Jersey   4

Headline News   8

Missing Word Quiz   9

A First for Alex   10

Legends 3   14

Blue Heaven   17

The Scottish Cup Final & the Old Firm   18

More Than Enough, Peter Lovenkrands   20

The Scottish Cup Campaign 2002   24

The Scottish Cup Final 2002   26

It's a Rangers Final Fact   32

Kiev Samovar 1987   34

Rangers and the Scottish Cup Quiz   36

Old Firm Quiz   37

The Benfica Caravel 1948   38

Team Rangers   40

Team Rangers Quiz   54

The Murray Years   55

Rangers in Europe Quiz   56

Rangers True? Rangers False?   58

Quiz Answers   62

PLAYING FOR THE JERSEY

CIS INSURANCE CUP
SEMI-FINAL
5 February 2002

RANGERS 2   CELTIC 1

Lovenkrands (45 mins.) Konterman (105 mins.)

Alex McLeish headed for Hampden that early February Tuesday evening – and his first major date with destiny – in the knowledge that none of the previous four managers of Glasgow Rangers had tasted defeat in their first encounter with Celtic. Walter Smith, Graeme Souness and Jock Wallace had all secured victory in their initial clashes with the team in green whilst Dick Advocaat's side had earned a 0-0 draw in the Dutchman's introductory Old Firm derby back in September 1998. Welcome to the show that never ends, Alex!

Although unbeaten in the SPL so far, this would be the toughest test yet for the new man at the helm and, in many ways, his real baptism. The pressure was certainly on him as Celtic had won the previous five encounters between these greatest of rivals. This time, however, it would be different.

Certainly the Parkhead side started the stronger of the two (and indeed could have been ahead early on) but Rangers were soon creating chances of their own with Arveladze, in particular, coming close in what was fast

becoming an incident packed game. The breakthrough eventually came just before the interval when the persistent Peter Lovenkrands (named in the senior Danish squad for the first time earlier that day) superbly squeezed the ball home despite Swede Mjallby having given the impression of being in control of their penalty box joust. The winger celebrated with a handstand as the 'follow-follow' brigade inside the national stadium bounced with delight.

The second half was no less dramatic and, after some 74 minutes, Celtic equalised with a bundled goal by their defender Balde. Within minutes of the restart, Rangers were awarded a penalty (when the same player fouled Lovenkrands in the box) but unfortunately striker Arveladze clipped the top of the bar with the resultant spot kick and the chance to regain the lead was lost. With no more goals in the regulation period, extra time would now decide the outcome of what was becoming a truly epic battle. By this time, many fans were of the opinion that it would take something really special to win this semi-final. And, boy, how right they were!

With the stadium clock showing 105 minutes played, Bert Konterman (a somewhat unlikely hero) struck a blistering thirty-yard drive that screamed past Douglas in the Celtic goal, leaving the 'Hoop' dream of record back-to-back trebles in ruin once and for all. Surely the best strike of the Dutchman's football career so far and, no doubt, a moment in time that the amiable chap will remember long after his playing days have come to an end. With a few choruses of that popular Ibrox ditty 'Where's your treble gone?' the lads on the terracing celebrated all the way to the final whistle and beyond. It had been quite a night for them.

On the field, the team spirit was there for all to see with everyone simply playing for the jersey. Three months later, in the Scottish Cup Final with Celtic, any lingering questions about their commitment to the cause would be answered the very same way.

Rangers: Klos, Ricksen, Moore, Amoruso, Konterman, Numan, Ferguson, Caniggia, De Boer, Arveladze and Lovenkrands.

HEADLINE NEWS

RANGERS MADE THE FOLLOWING FOOTBALL HEADLINES DURING SEASON 2001/02.

WHAT WAS THE OCCASION?
THE CLUE IS IN THE DATE!

'Konterman crusade to convert doubters' Daily Mail, 13.8.01

'Full Flo turns tide for Rangers' Sunday Herald, 23.9.01

'The Boy Dane Damn Good' Sunday Mail, 5.5.02

'Memory Man' Daily Mail, 19.10.01

'Agony then Ecstasy' Daily Record, 7.12.01

'I'm determined to do it my way' Daily Mail, 12.12.01

'Sauzee fails to rewrite tale of a century' Sunday Herald, 27.1.02

'K.O.nterman' Daily Record, 6.2.02

'Outplayed, out-thought, outfought' Glasgow Herald, 6.5.02

'Lovin' it, Lovin' it, Loven it' Daily Record, 6.5.02

HEADLINE NEWS

ANSWERS ON PAGE 62

MISSING WORD QUIZ

FILL IN THE NAME OF THE MISSING RANGER FROM SEASON 2001/02 FOOTBALL HEADLINES. THE CLUE IS IN THE DATE!

'The ------ Final' Daily Record, 6.5.02

'Show-stopper ----- a superior specimen' Daily Mail, 10.10.01

'-------' insists he has a part to play at Rangers' The Herald, 18.5.02

'----- spares McLeish blushes' Sunday Herald, 3.2.02

'-------- stays cool to keep Rangers in hunt' Daily Mail, 22.2.02

'Forfar beg for mercy but ----- preys on' Daily Mail, 25.2.02

'Sorry Saints can't stem the ---' Daily Mail, 7.3.02

'---- keeps big guns from cracking under Ayr pressure' Daily Mail, 18.3.02

'------- takes first step' Glasgow Herald, 18.3.02

'--------- return puts Partick to the sword' Daily Mail, 25.3.02

ANSWERS ON PAGE 62

A FIRST FOR ALEX

CIS INSURANCE CUP FINAL
17 MARCH 2002

RANGERS 4   AYR UNITED 0

Flo (44 mins.), Ferguson (49 mins.),
Caniggia (75, 90 mins.)

After disposing of SPL stalwarts Kilmarnock and Hibernian along the way, nobody could begrudge Ayr United their place in the CIS Insurance Cup Final of 2002. Indeed, after the flying Dane Peter Lovenkrands had missed an early chance, it was the First Division outfit who made most of the running in the initial stages of the game. Strikers McLaughlin and Grady were stopped by blocking tackles from Tony Vidmar and Barry Ferguson respectively before Stefan Klos pulled off one of the saves of the season to deny ex-Celt McLaughlin again. **Obviously, the outsiders were not at Hampden simply to make up the numbers but, then again, neither was 'Man of the Match' Claudio Caniggia.**

Just before the break, after a superb mazy run which left the Ayr defenders turning circles, the Argentine legend released a delightful ball to Tore

Andre Flo who netted from the tightest of angles. Following, no doubt, a few well chosen words from Alex McLeish at half-time, it was a far more purposeful Rangers side that re-appeared for the second period and, virtually right at the start, were awarded a penalty after Russell Latapy was fouled in the box. Barry Ferguson, coolness personified, slotted effortlessly home.

The Ibrox side's dominance was emphasised further still when Caniggia side-footed a Neil McCann cross into the net (with some fifteen minutes remaining) before the same player claimed his double, right at the end, with a close range header from Fernando Ricksen's accurate penalty box delivery. **The time had come for Barry Ferguson to lift his first trophy as captain of Rangers.**

Although Alex McLeish had played in seven League Cup Finals with Aberdeen (and won two winners' medals himself), this time the scenario was entirely different. As manager of Glasgow Rangers, and after just three months at the club, silverware was in his possession for the very first time. In the eyes of those who follow, the fact that the scalp of Celtic had been taken along the way made the occasion just that little bit sweeter.

Rangers: Klos, Ricksen, Vidmar, Amoruso, Numan, Konterman, Ferguson, Latapy, Caniggia, Flo and Lovenkrands.

LEGENDS THREE

JIMMY MILLAR   **RALPH BRAND**   **DAVIE WILSON**

Manager Scot Symon's wonderful side of the early 1960s boasted a trio of top goal scorers that have all become club legends. Between them, they amassed an astonishing 521 goals for Rangers and, at the time, the mere mention of their names was enough to strike fear in opposition defences everywhere. They were, as many fathers will surely know, strikers Jimmy Millar/Ralph Brand and winger Davie Wilson.

JIMMY MILLAR

Certain players hold a special place in the hearts of a whole generation of fans. Jimmy Millar - fearless, daring and quite superb in the air (despite being only five and a half feet tall) - is one such individual. Actually a half-back with Dunfermline, Scot Symon paid £5000 for his services in January 1955 but then a bizarre twist of fate changed his Ibrox career. Due to an injury to Max Murray during a friendly tour game with Danish outfit Staevnet in May 1959, Millar was moved to centre-forward for the second-half and duly netted four times. A striker was born!

He gained almost legendary status during the Scottish Cup run of 1960 when, firstly, his headed goal (from all of sixteen yards!) equalised against Celtic in the semi-final. The player then claimed two more in the 4-1 replay victory before netting both in the 2-0 final triumph over Kilmarnock. Millar was also top scorer in the league that year with 21 conversions to his name.

By Season 1960/61, his deadly partnership with the inimitable Ralph Brand had been forged and, between them, the duo would go on to claim over 360 goals in the true blue of Rangers. Indeed, it was this very partnership that eventually secured the Scottish Cup of 1964 when both of them scored in the last few minutes to deny Dundee 3-1 in one of the classic Hampden encounters. In the latter days of his Ibrox career, Millar collected Scottish Cup medal number five (back in his 'old' half-back position) when Celtic were beaten 1-0 courtesy of Kai Johansen's rifled shot in the April 1966 replay.

Jimmy Millar, with 160 goals to his credit, will always be remembered as one of the most inspirational centre-forwards to have worn the colours.

RALPH BRAND

All Ralph Brand wanted to be was a footballer. First spotted by manager Bill Struth in a 1952 schoolboy international, the youngster was signed on provisional forms before, some two and a half years later, netting twice on his Rangers debut when Kilmarnock were crushed 6-0 in the league game of November 1954.

After his National Service, the player scored 11 times in 22 league games during Season 1957/58. Twelve months on, the statistics revealed only 3 more games played but an additional 10 goals in total. In the first official outing of Season 1959/60, the blossoming partnership with Jimmy Millar was already paying dividends - between them, the duo netted five times as Hibernian were swamped 6-1 in the League Cup. By Season 1960/61, the Millar/Brand partnership was in full flow and claimed 33 league strikes as Rangers completed a League and League Cup double. When Dundee were beaten 3-1 on April 25, 1964, Brand entered the record books as the first footballer to score in three successive Scottish Cup Finals following his goals against St. Mirren (2-0, 21.4.62) and Celtic (3-0, 15.5.63) the previous years. He actually hit a double in the Old Firm final of 1963. Additionally, the striker netted six times in seven Cup Finals with the 'Light Blues' and was never on a losing side!

In May 1961, Ralph Brand was a member of the Ibrox team that became the first British club to reach the final of a European competition - the Cup Winners' Cup.

He not only scored in every round of the tournament but also claimed a hat-trick in the quarter-final tie with the Germans of Borussia Moenchengladbach. In total, Brand's Ibrox career would net an astonishing 206 goals.

DAVIE WILSON

In the eyes of many, Davie Wilson was the finest left-winger to wear the blue since the incomparable 'Wee Blue Devil' Alan Morton, back in the 1920s. Having arrived at Ibrox as a teenager (via Baillieston Juniors), the youngster scored on his fourth first-team outing against Motherwell in March 1957 as Rangers won 5-2 on their way to retaining the League Championship.

In Season 1960/61, Wilson was second-top scorer (behind Ralph Brand) with 19 goals to his credit from 34 games. He then became the only post-war player to net six times in one competitive game when Falkirk were thrashed 7-1 at Brockville on March 17, 1962. Not surprisingly, the record still stands to this day. His following month goal in the Scottish Cup Final against St. Mirren (2-0, 21.4.62) was complimented, just over one year later, by another strike when Old Firm rivals Celtic were defeated 3-0 at Hampden in the replayed final of May 1963.

In the dark blue of Scotland, few have forgotten his performance against England at Wembley in 1963. Following captain (and fellow Ranger) Eric Caldow's broken leg in just six minutes, Wilson slotted into the left full-back position as if to the manor born and played a stormer. Scotland recorded a 2-1 victory, with another Govan legend, Jim Baxter, netting both. The previous year at Hampden, Davie himself had scored as Scotland registered their first win in official internationals against England in some 25 years.

Davie Wilson totalled 155 goals during his Ibrox career. Not bad for a winger!

Footnote: Jimmy Millar, Ralph Brand and Davie Wilson all scored at Celtic Park in September 1960 when Rangers won 5-1, the club's biggest ever win in the east end of Glasgow.

BLUE HEAVEN

RANGERS – THE HONOURS

SCOTTISH LEAGUE CHAMPIONSHIPS (49)

1891, 1899, 1900, 1901, 1902, 1911, 1912, 1913, 1918, 1920, 1921,
1923, 1924, 1925, 1927, 1928, 1929, 1930, 1931, 1933, 1934, 1935,
1937, 1939, 1947, 1949, 1950, 1953, 1956, 1957, 1959, 1961, 1963,
1964, 1975, 1976, 1978, 1987, 1989, 1990, 1991, 1992, 1993, 1994,
1995, 1996, 1997, 1999, 2000.

SCOTTISH CUPS (30)

1894, 1897, 1898, 1903, 1928, 1930, 1932, 1934, 1935, 1936, 1948,
1949, 1950, 1953, 1960, 1962, 1963, 1964, 1966, 1973, 1976, 1978,
1979, 1981, 1992, 1993, 1996, 1999, 2000, 2002,

SCOTTISH LEAGUE CUPS (22)

1946/47, 1948/49, 1960/61, 1961/62, 1963/64, 1964/65, 1970/71,
1975/76, 1977/78, 1978/79, 1981/82, 1983/84, 1984/85, 1986/87,
1987/88, 1988/89, 1990/91, 1992/93, 1993/94, 1996/97, 1998/99,
2001/02.

EUROPEAN CUP WINNERS' CUP

Winners 1972
Runners up 1961, 1967.

THE VICTORY CUP 1946

THE SCOTTISH CUP FINAL AND THE OLD FIRM

Season 2001/02 was the 15th occasion that Rangers have met Celtic in the Scottish Cup Final. Results (and scorers) as follows:

Season 1893/94 Rangers 3   Celtic 1
McCreadie, Barker, McPherson

Season 1898/99 Celtic 2   Rangers 0

Season 1903/04 Celtic 3   Rangers 2
Speedie (2)

Season 1908/09 Rangers 1   Celtic 1 (replay after 2-2 draw)
Gordon
(Trophy withheld following a pitch invasion after the drawn replay)

Season 1927/28 Rangers 4   Celtic 0
Meiklejohn, McPhail, Archibald (2)

Season 1962/63 Rangers 3   Celtic 0 (replay after 1-1 draw)
Brand (2), Wilson

Season 1965/66 Rangers 1   Celtic 0 (replay after 0-0 draw)
Johansen

Season 1968/69 Celtic 4   Rangers 0

Season 1970/71 Celtic 2   Rangers 1 (replay after 1-1 draw)
Craig og

Season 1972/73 Rangers 3   Celtic 2
Parlane, Conn, Forsyth

Season 1976/77 Celtic 1   Rangers 0

Season 1979/80   Celtic 1   Rangers 0   (after extra time)

Season 1988/89   Celtic 1   Rangers 0

Season 1998/99   Rangers 1   Celtic 0
  Wallace

Season 2001/02   Rangers 3   Celtic 2
  Lovenkrands (2), Ferguson

MORE THAN ENOUGH
PETER LOVENKRANDS

Before Season 2001/02, the last Ranger to score twice in an Old Firm Scottish Cup Final was the legendary Ralph Brand when Celtic (following a 1-1 draw) were beaten 3-0 in May 1963. By matching that rather special feat in the Cup Final of 2002, Ibrox immortality beckoned for Dane Peter Lovenkrands whose performance that day in the Hampden sun brought memories flooding back of another Prince from Denmark, the great Brian Laudrup.

Some three months earlier, again at the National Stadium, the 22-year-old winger more than played his part in the CIS Insurance Cup semi-final when Celtic were earlier victims. A thorn in the side of the green rearguard for the whole game, his late first-half goal combined both opportunism and perseverance despite defender Mjallby's close protection of the ball. It should not be forgotten that his lightning pace also earned Rangers a penalty that night although Georgian international Shota Arveladze failed to take advantage from the spot.

In the UEFA Cup tie against Feyenoord in Rotterdam, Peter's speed was again put to the best of use and should have earned the 'Light Blues' a penalty when, during the early part of this crucial encounter, his marker Paauwe fouled him in the box. As there

was no score at that stage, a converted penalty would have completely changed the complexion of the game and, probably, the actual outcome.

Of course, it has been the eye-catching performances of Lovenkrands (who arrived in Glasgow from AB Copenhagen for some £1.5 million despite interest from Newcastle) in the tense encounters with great rivals Celtic that have made the headlines in Season 2001/02. No wonder the scouts of other major clubs are taking note - five goals in the last four Old firm clashes of that period are impressive statistics in anyone's book! Special mention, naturally, must be made of his double on Scottish Cup Final Day when manager Alex McLeish played him through the middle as Rangers' main striker. The first, almost immediately after Celtic had taken the lead, was a left-foot shot that beat Douglas at his near post and the second (as if you didn't know!) was a downward header from Neil McCann's pinpoint cross right at the end that ensured the old trophy would be bearing blue and white ribbons some minutes later.

There were many heroes that day but only one could claim to have equalled the performance by a striker almost forty years previously. In his Ibrox days, Ralph Brand netted 206 goals. It remains to be seen what total Peter Lovenkrands will accumulate during his period in Govan but, in the early summer of 2002, those two beauties from May 4 were more than enough for all friends of Rangers.

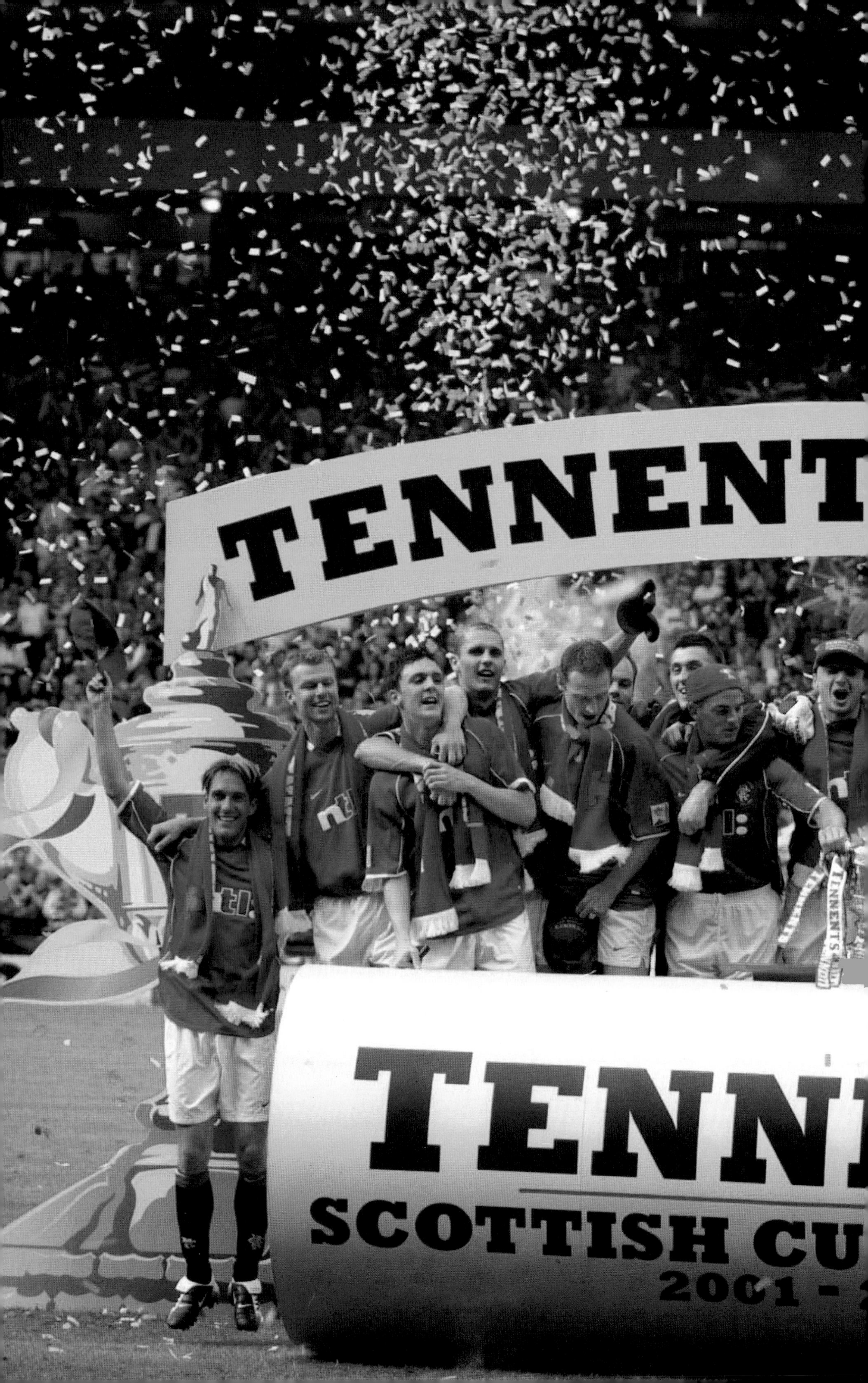
TENNENT
TENN
SCOTTISH CU
2001 -

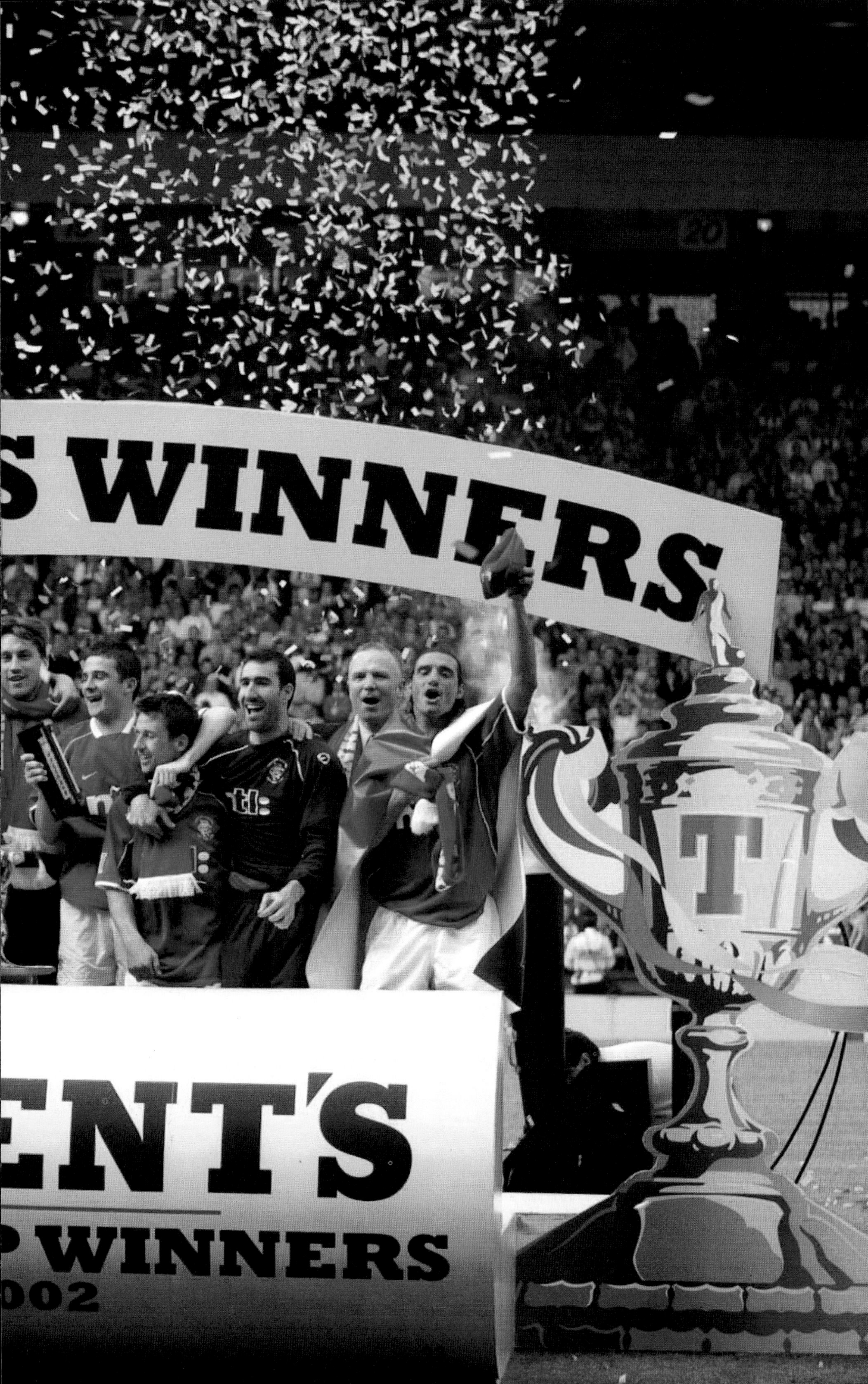
S WINNERS
ENT'S
P WINNERS
002

THE SCOTTISH CUP
CAMPAIGN 2002

Rangers 3 - Berwick Rangers 0

It all began in late January when Rangers entered the competition (at the third-round stage) and were drawn away to their namesakes in Berwick. Rather famously, the English outfit had been 1-0 conquerors of the Ibrox side in the same competition way back in 1967 when future 'Light Blue' legend Jock Wallace was the Shielfield Park goalkeeper. After being held to a disappointing 0-0 draw over the border (although a sixties type shock was never really on the cards), progress to the next round was achieved following a 3-0 Govan victory before a surprisingly low home crowd of less than 18,000. Second-half goals from Lorenzo Amoruso (a thunderous 35 yard strike), Bert Konterman and Shota Arveladze ensured a Glasgow date with Hibernian, five days later on January 26.

Rangers: Klos, Ross, Konterman, Amoruso, Vidmar, Hughes, Ferguson, Latapy, McCann, Arveladze and Mols.

Rangers 4 - Hibernian 1

The Edinburgh side had not lifted the Scottish Cup since 1902 and Rangers 4-1 fourth-round demolition of the Leith outfit ensured that this record would remain in place for at least another year. Two goals from Tore Andre Flo (22 so far for the season) and one apiece from Peter Lovenkrands and substitute Billy Dodds sent the fans home happy, many already thinking about the road north, Forfar bridies and a quarter-final date at Station Park.

Rangers: Klos, Ricksen, Moore, Amoruso, Vidmar, Konterman, Ferguson, De Boer, Arveladze, Flo and Lovenkrands.

Rangers 6 - Forfar 0

Although Forfar showed plenty of endeavour, the huge gulf between the SPL and the Second Division was reflected in the 6-0 scoreline. Fans' favourite Billy Dodds scored in the very first minute before completing his hat-trick (despite a penalty miss) right at the end. Other names on the scoresheet that day were Arveladze (2) and Kanchelskis.

Rangers: Klos, Ricksen, Amoruso, Vidmar, Numan, Kanchelskis, Hughes, Ferguson, McCann, Dodds and Arveladze.

Rangers 3 - Partick Thistle 0

First Division Champions Partick Thistle were opponents in the semi-final at the National Stadium on March 24 before a crowd of 32,000. Starting only his second game in over seven months, German Christian Nerlinger netted twice in each half of this Hampden encounter, deservedly winning the 'Man-of-the-Match' prize with an excellent central midfield display. Barry Ferguson played a captain's part and claimed Rangers' third (in the 3-0 triumph) as the follow-followers prepared themselves for an epic confrontation with League Champions Celtic in the final.

Rangers: Klos, Ricksen, Malcolm, Amoruso, Vidmar, Kanchelskis, Nerlinger, Ferguson, McCann, Caniggia and Flo.

MEMORIES ARE MADE OF THIS
SCOTTISH CUP FINAL, 4 MAY 2002
RANGERS 3   CELTIC 2

Lovenkrands (21, 90 mins.) Ferguson (68 mins.)

All Rangers fans of a certain age remember, with more than just a little emotion, the Centenary Scottish Cup Final of 1973 when Celtic were beaten 3-2 in a dramatic showdown with Princess Alexandra in attendance amongst the 122,714 spectators. Nearly thirty years on (in the year of the Queen's Golden Jubilee but before a crowd of less than half that previous figure), the final of 2002 was destined to become an integral part of Ibrox legend in much the same way as that classic encounter in the seventies.

The game started well for the 'Light Blues' but, with Claudio Caniggia off the field having treatment following an illegal Sutton challenge, Hartson nodded home to open the scoring for Celtic whilst Rangers were down to ten men. Within two minutes, however, 'Gers drew level when Peter Lovenkrands rifled a low shot past Douglas (after quickly turning away from defenders Mjallby and Sutton) to become the first player to net against Celtic in the Scottish Cup that season. It remained 1-1 as half-time approached.

Despite starting the second period strongly, the 'Light Blues' fell behind again when Balde's powerful header beat Stefan Klos from close range. However, this was a game that Rangers never looked like losing and the Ibrox side, with the majestic Barry Ferguson orchestrating everything from midfield, continued to play with complete assurance as Celtic began to wilt. After Ferguson had come close and hit the post with a blistering drive, his wonderful 'Beckham-style' free-kick from some 22 yards brought his side level with just over twenty minutes still to play.

Continuing to push forward, justice was served deep into injury time when Neil McCann's delightful cross into the box was headed downwards by Lovenkrands after the young Dane had summoned up the last of his energy to meet the ball in the six-yard box. He had just become the first Ranger in nearly forty years to claim two in an Old Firm Scottish Cup Final. Celtic were well and truly beaten and, in truth, there could be no excuses from the

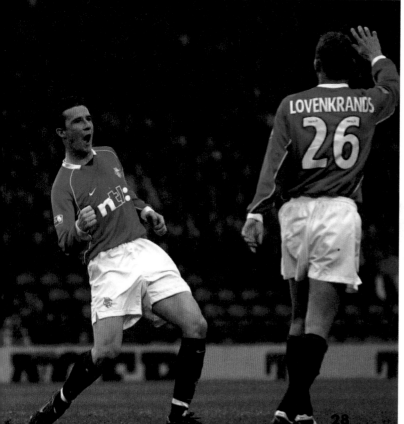

other side of the city as by far the better team had won on the day.

By denying Martin O'Neill's side their first back-to-back League and Scottish Cup double since the days of Jock Stein back in 1972, manager Alex McLeish had now lifted two of the three domestic trophies (in just 29 games at the Ibrox helm) and, rather importantly, witnessed the league champions not only outplayed but also outfought by his team of winners. That would stay with him, and all those of a blue persuasion, for the longest of times.

Rangers: Klos, Ross, Moore, Amoruso, Numan, Ricksen, Ferguson, De Boer, Caniggia, Lovenkrands and McCann.

Each time a European final has been played at Hampden Park, Rangers have lifted the Scottish Cup. YES, IT'S A FACT!

When Kilmarnock were beaten 2-0 in the final of 1960, Real Madrid met Eintracht Frankfurt in the European Cup Final in Glasgow. Two years later (with Fiorentina and Atletico Madrid in town to contest the Cup Winners' Cup Final), the 'Light Blues' defeated St. Mirren by the same 2-0 score to take the trophy. When Kai Johansen's famous strike sealed victory over Celtic in 1966, Liverpool and Borussia Dortmund fought out the final of the Cup Winners' Cup at the National Stadium and, then, Rangers' 3-1 defeat of Hearts was the forerunner of the 1976 Bayern Munich/St. Etienne European Cup Final. Finally, of course, Real Madrid were due to meet Bayer Leverkusen in the Champions League showdown of May 2002 shortly after Rangers had famously beaten Celtic 3-2. YES, IT'S A FACT!

For the first time in 43 games and an incredible nine years, on Scottish Cup Final Day 2002, Rangers became the first Old Firm side to win this derby encounter after losing the first goal. YES, IT'S A FACT!

Of course, Rangers beat Ayr United in the CIS Insurance Cup Final of 2002. Did you know that the last time these teams met in the same competition, the trophy also returned to Ibrox? Back in Season 1998/99, goals from Gabriel Amato and Charlie Miller disposed of Ayr 2-0 in an earlier round before St. Johnstone were beaten 2-1 in the final played at Celtic Park.

YES, IT'S A FACT!

Christian Nerlinger has a 100% cup final record, having only played in one such occasion back in his homeland when Bayern Munich defeated MSV Duisburg to lift the German trophy. YES, IT'S A FACT!

Legendary goalscorer Ralph Brand played in seven finals with Rangers (scoring in every one bar the League Cup Final of 1963) and was never on a losing side. The games were:

1960 League Cup Final (Rangers 2 Kilmarnock 0), 1961 League Cup Final (Rangers 3 Hearts 1), 1962 Scottish Cup Final (Rangers 2 St. Mirren 0), 1963 Scottish Cup Final (Rangers 3 Celtic 0), 1963 League Cup Final (Rangers 5 Morton 0), 1964 Scottish Cup Final (Rangers 3 Dundee 1) and the 1964 League Cup Final (Rangers 2 Celtic 1). YES, IT'S A FACT!

IT'S A RANGERS 'FINAL' FACT!

KIEV SAMOVAR 1987

Rangers played Dynamo Kiev in the first round of the European Cup in September 1987 after player/manager Graeme Souness had led the Ibrox club to their first Scottish league title in nine years the previous season. Back in the late eighties, the Russians were considered by many to be just about the finest club side in the world – borne out by the fact that they formed the backbone of the Soviet national side in those days. Although Rangers played extremely well in the first leg (before a massive crowd of 100,000 in the Ukraine), the game was decided from the penalty spot in favour of the home side. Indeed, it was Alexei Mikhailitchenko (a future Ranger) who netted the only goal of the ninety minutes. Defender Oleg Kuznetsov also impressed during the game and he too would duly arrive in Scotland to sign for the club, albeit some three years after these events.

More than a little controversy surrounded the return leg in Glasgow before a ball was even kicked. Graeme Souness, aware of the Russians' style of play, had the width of the pitch reduced by one or two yards thus restricting their game plan. Even although this was naturally within the rules, they were not pleased - to say the least!

The atmosphere and noise that night was quite remarkable as the follow-followers made the stadium vibrate in anticipation of a great occasion. The players responded in kind and goals from Mark Falco (in the first-half) and Ally McCoist (early in the second) sealed Rangers' passage to the next round with a famous 2-0 victory. To this day, the occasion is still remembered as one of the great Ibrox European nights.

First Leg 16.9.87   Dynamo Kiev 1 Rangers 0

Rangers: Woods, Nicholl, Phillips, Roberts, Souness, Butcher, D.Ferguson, Cohen, McCoist, Durrant and McGregor.

Second Leg 30.9.87   Rangers 2 Dynamo Kiev 0

Falco (23), McCoist (49)

Rangers: Woods, Nicholl, Phillips, McGregor, Souness, Butcher, Francis, Falco, McCoist, Durrant and Cohen.

RANGERS AND THE SCOTTISH CUP QUIZ

1) Who scored Rangers' first and last goals in the Scottish Cup campaign of 2002?

2) Apart from 2002, in what other year did Rangers lift the Scottish Cup after defeating Celtic 3-2 in the final?

3) Name the top scorer for the 'Light Blues' in the Scottish Cup of 2002.

4) In 1996, who claimed a hat-trick in the final, becoming the first player to achieve this feat since 1972?

5) How many times have Rangers beaten Celtic in the Scottish Cup Final?

6) In Round 1 of the 1933/34 competition, Blairgowrie were crushed 14-2. Jimmy Fleming created a club record that day with how many goals?

7) Peter Lovenkrands only scored in the final of the 2002 competition. True or false?

8) In the 1992/93 final, it was the youngest player on the park who opened the scoring. Can you name him

9) Name the only two outfield players who made the starting line-up in every round of the 2002 Scottish Cup.

10) Back in 1966, a fellow countryman of Peter Lovenkrands became the first foreign player to win a Scottish Cup medal. Who was he?

ANSWERS ON PAGE 62

READY

OLD FIRM QUIZ

1) True or false – Rangers have won the Scottish League Championship more times than Celtic?

2) In how many competitions did Peter Lovenkrands score against Celtic last season?

3) What is Rangers biggest winning margin in the Scottish Cup Final encounters with their Old Firm rivals?

4) In 1963, for the first time in thirty-five years, Rangers met Celtic in the final of The Scottish Cup. What was the score?

5) Name the legendary Rangers captain who claimed the extra-time winner in the League Cup Final of Season 1990/91.

6) Who scored a double at Celtic Park on Championship Day 1999?

7) Name the player who made a crucial goaline clearance in the first minute of the 2002 CIS Insurance Cup semi-final?

8) Who scored the goal at Easter Road in March 1975 that finally ended Celtic's domination of the domestic title scene?

9) How many fans were officially at Hampden in May 1973 when Rangers beat Celtic 3-2 in the Centenary Scottish Cup Final?

10) How many times have you watched the video of the 2002 Scottish Cup Final?

ANSWERS
ON
PAGE 62

THE BENFICA CARAVEL 1948

Rangers' first competitive game in Europe was against Nice of France in the European Cup tie of October 1956. Some eight years before that special occasion, the great manager William Struth took his team to Portugal to play champions Benfica of Lisbon in a friendly match in February 1948.

Of course, in those days air travel was somewhat longer and more complicated. The team flew out from Prestwick in a chartered twin-engined Dakota that had to land in Bordeaux for refuelling before taking off again and completing the flight to Lisbon. Total journey time – 11 hours!

Prior to kick-off, the Portugese champions presented Rangers with a small pig for mascot duty but captain Jock 'Tiger' Shaw, perhaps understandably, refused point blank to lead the animal out in advance of his team.

The match itself was viewed by some 60,000 locals who saw their visitors net three times in the last seven minutes of the game for an impressive 3-0 victory.

Jimmy Duncanson claimed two and the legendary Willie Thornton the other. *Incidentally, the following season, Rangers would become the first team to lift Scotland's domestic treble of League, League Cup and Scottish Cup.*

Even romance was in the air that night as Willie Waddell, another Rangers great both as player and manager, met his future wife on the trip. She was a flight stewardess on the outward and return journeys!

Rangers: Brown, Young, Shaw, McColl, Woodburn, Cox, Waddell, Gillick, Thornton, Duncanson and Caskie.

TEAM RANGERS

THE MANAGER
ALEX McLEISH

Arriving at the club as team manager in December 2001, Alex McLeish guided his new charges to two of the three Scottish domestic honours on offer in his first (part) season at the helm. Both the CIS Insurance Cup and the Scottish Cup were back in the Ibrox Trophy Room following final victories over Ayr United (4-0, 17.3.02) and Celtic (3-2, 4.5.02) respectively. After negotiations with chairman David Murray (in the same month as that now legendary triumph over Old Firm rivals Celtic), Alex McLeish agreed an extension to his current contract which will now see him at Ibrox until at least year 2004.

THE PLAYERS
STEFAN KLOS

Stefan Klos was one of the heroes when Celtic were beaten 2-1 in the CIS Insurance Cup semi-final at Hampden in February 2002. The German goalkeeper (proud owner of a Champions' League medal won with Borussia Dortmund) was in superlative form that night and kept Rangers in the game early on with a series of important saves. Two in particular (from midfielder Petrov and striker Larsson in the first seven minutes of the match) were simply world class. Few will ever forget another quite remarkable stop in the final of that same competition when Klos somehow managed to claw a McLaughlin chip shot out of the air with the score still 0-0 and the game evenly balanced between Rangers and Ayr United. Apart from the penultimate and ultimate league games of Season 2001/02 (when Allan McGregor deputised), Stefan Klos was an ever-present and started a total of 57 times both home and abroad.

MAURICE ROSS

Many friends of Rangers felt that the young defender 'came of age' in the 2001/02 period, especially with regard to his extremely impressive performances against Celtic in the latter part of the season. In both the 1-1 April draw in the east end of Glasgow and the Scottish Cup Final triumph the following month, Ross was really quite immense on the right side of the field, playing and tackling like a veteran of numerous Old Firm campaigns. The youngster (who had suffered a bad ankle injury back in January 2001 whilst touring Australia with the under-21 side) totalled 24 starts for the 'Light Blues' last year. Scotland national team boss Berti Vogts awarded him his first Scotland cap in May 2002 for the tour game with South Korea - albeit on the left side of the park.

KEVIN MUSCAT

Fiercely competitive with the 'never say die' attitude of a real committed winner, twenty-eight-year-old defender Kevin Muscat arrived at Ibrox from Molyneux (home of Wolverhampton Wanderers) in the summer of 2002 under freedom of contract, adding an additional presence of steel to the blue rearguard. The unyielding full back first played with fellow Ranger Craig Moore in the Australian Under-20s before they both graduated to the full national side some years later.

TEAM RANGERS

FERNANDO RICKSEN

Joint-second only to Stefan Klos in the appearances chart for Season 2001/02 (with a total of 46 outings), Fernando Ricksen ended the year with a tireless display at Hampden in the Scottish Cup Final when the Dutchman successfully filled fellow countryman Bert Konterman's midfield holding role for Rangers. Most fans who doubted the wisdom of his signing initially have since been converted and the versatile player has indeed come a long way, in their eyes, since his first appearance against the team in green when he was substituted less than twenty-five minutes into the game, back in August 2000! Ricksen netted five times last term, keeping the best for last when he unleashed an absolute screamer from some twenty-two yards near the end of the 3-0 Ibrox dismantling of Motherwell in February 2002.

ARTHUR NUMAN

Dick Advocaat's captain at PSV Eindhoven for four years, the cultured left full-back turned out 43 times in the blue during Season 2001/02. Although his name was only on one league strike throughout that period, most fans agree that it was, without doubt, one of the goals of the season. In the Old Firm championship game of March 2002, Celtic led 1-0 at half-time on a very windy Ibrox day. Some fifteen minutes into the second period, McCann fed Numan thirty-five yards out and the Dutchman, seemingly with little effort, released a thunderbolt strike that flew past Douglas into the far corner of his net and tied the game. The words 'Jorg' and 'Albertz' sprang to mind! A constant threat going forward, the defender is one of the few players in Scotland able to curb the attacking menace of Celtic's Didier Agathe and rarely has a bad game when in opposition to him.

ROBERT MALCOLM

Alex McLeish gave the youngster his first start of last season in the 5-0 Govan demolition of Kilmarnock, March 2002. The 21-year-old defender returned the compliment with an impressive showing alongside Lorenzo Amoruso at the heart of the Ibrox backline. After that, apart from Scottish Cup Final Day when the experienced Craig Moore returned to face Celtic, Malcolm was an ever-present right up until the end of the campaign, including the last game at Dunfermline in May. Earlier that season, manager Alex Smith had tried to take the player to Dundee United (and, no doubt, guaranteed first-team football) but Robert, declining the offer, decided to remain with his boyhood heroes and fight for a place in the team.

MICHAEL BALL

Signed from Everton for £6.5 million, the English defender made his first appearance for Rangers in the CIS Insurance cup tie with Airdrie in October 2001, impressing the fans with his cool, calm and confident play. The following week, on European duty in the clash with Moscow Dynamo, his twenty-five yard free-kick gave the Ibrox side a two nil advantage at a most crucial time in this UEFA Cup encounter. That powerful left foot was put to good advantage again only three days later when the 'Light Blues' travelled to Perth looking for SPL points. Early in the second period, Ball's searing thirty-yard drive struck the underside of the crossbar thus enabling striker Shota Arveladze to net the rebound and open the scoring in what was proving to be a difficult game. Sadly, due to serious injury, his last appearance of the season was in early December last year (away to Dundee) but hopefully Michael will be back fully fit in the near future.

TEAM RANGERS

BERT KONTERMAN

Injury meant that the amiable Dutchman missed the last eight games of Season 2001/02 including, of course, the Scottish Cup Final. Prior to that, he appeared for Rangers 41 times and netted on five of those occasions in various league and cup matches. As well as a rare double in the SPL encounter with Dunfermline in Fife (4-1, 11.8.01), Konterman claimed vital goals in the one-off UEFA Cup tie with Anzhi Makhachkala in neutral Poland's Legia Warsaw Stadium (which finally ended that ongoing Dagestan dispute!) and the CIS Cup semi-final joust with Celtic. Of course, his explosively stunning strike in the aforementioned Old Firm cup game back in February 2002 is now the stuff of legend, ensuring a permanent place in the Ibrox Hall of Fame for the former farmer from Holland.

CRAIG MOORE

At home and abroad, all 'follow-followers' breathed a collective sigh of relief when defender Craig Moore finally returned to first-team action in the home game with Aberdeen on April 27, 2002. At least there was now a real possibility that the powerful Aussie would be fit enough to face the other half of the Old Firm (in particular strikers Larsson and Hartson) on Scottish Cup Final Day one week later. Indeed, it was during an earlier cup clash with Celtic back in February (the CIS Insurance semi-final encounter) that Moore had been originally crocked when he collided with Stefan Klos and landed awkwardly on the Hampden turf. His performance at the National Stadium on 4 May, three months later, was typically robust as he and fellow defender Lorenzo Amoruso kept the Celtic front men at bay for most of the ninety minutes thus ensuring a day to remember.

RONALD DE BOER

Another member of the Dutch brigade at Ibrox, midfielder Ronald de Boer started 30 times and claimed eight goals in Season 2001/02. Both of his two European strikes during that period came in the Round 2 UEFA Cup games with Moscow Dynamo when he netted home (a header from Claudio Reyna's free-kick some ten minutes before the end) and away in the 3-1 and 4-1 victories respectively. In addition, on SPL duty, he claimed a double at East End Park, Dunfermline when the 'Light Blues' recorded an impressive 4-2 win in late January 2002. De Boer, signed from Barcelona for some £4.5 million in August 2000, has a football pedigree second to none in Scotland, having not only won a Champions' League winner's medal but also been an integral part of the fabulous Ajax side that both won (in 1995) and lost (in 1996, albeit on penalties) the European Cup.

STEPHEN HUGHES

In the early summer of 2002, after Stephen Hughes had agreed an extended Ibrox deal that will keep this young gem of a talent in Glasgow until at least year 2007, manager Alex McLeish was quoted as saying the following in reference to his midfielder: 'I first saw him as a 16-year-old and he struck me as someone who could control the game. He is energetic, gets forward, sprays passes and looks a natural-born footballer.' Earlier last season, many fans rightly suggested that the midfield section of the team was more than somewhat lacking since the departures of Giovanni van Bronckhorst, Tugay Kerimoglu and Jorg Albertz. Long-term injury to Christian Nerlinger and Claudio Reyna's subsequent move to Sunderland and the Premiership (in December of last year) were additional blows. Thankfully, circumstances are rather different now and the manager can select from, amongst others, Barry Ferguson, Mikel Arteta, a fit again Nerlinger and young Stephen himself, offering a mouthwatering blend of youth and experience in this vital area of the park.

TEAM RANGERS

MIKEL ARTETA

When class European outfit Paris St Germain drew 0-0 with Rangers in the UEFA Cup tie of late November 2001, a young Spaniard caught the eye as he orchestrated most of his side's attacking moves on an extremely cold Govan evening. Two weeks later, in the French capital, Mikel Arteta was again their most effective playmaker (and not a soft touch either!) in the return leg which was eventually won dramatically from the penalty spot by Dick Advocaat's side. Fast forward to May 2002 and that same very impressive youngster (an Under-21 international) signs on the dotted line for Rangers with £6 million heading south to Spain and the purse of Barcelona in exchange. The midfielder had, in fact, been on loan to PSG when he faced the 'Light Blues' the previous year and now, despite earlier strong interest from the French for his signature, chose to continue his football development in Scotland. Certainly no friend of Rangers was going to question that decision!

CHRISTIAN NERLINGER

Having spent most of Season 2001/02 on the treatment table, the German international returned to the fray in March for the 5-0 league destruction of Kilmarnock at Ibrox. There was no doubt that the midfielder had been sorely missed after starting his Rangers career with goals and a veritable bang in his first two games against both European (NK Maribor 3-0, 25.7.01) and Scottish opposition (Aberdeen 3-0, 28.7.01). Sadly, Nerlinger only played one more game (against Maribor again) before a foot injury struck and he was out of action for over seven months. Four days after his return to the side in that crushing encounter with the SPL team from Ayrshire, he was 'Man of the Match' in the Scottish Cup semi-final with Partick Thistle when his double strike on a Sunday afternoon (he netted two of three in the 3-0 triumph) eased his side through to a later date with Celtic at the same venue. The midfielder's overall performance was really quite magnificent, acting in tandem with midfield maestro Barry Ferguson who, incidentally, claimed the 'icing' third of the game near the end.

Winger Neil McCann was one of the three Rangers players who netted hat-tricks in Season 2001/02 - the other two being attackers Tore Andre Flo and Billy Dodds. His personal threesome (comprising of a header and two strikes) came in the March 2002 visit of Kilmarnock to Ibrox when the 'Light Blues' were in devastating form, hitting a high five without reply. Apart from his goals, McCann's overall wing play that night was quite exceptional. Some weeks later, in the penultimate league game of the season against Aberdeen, the winger achieved something that neither Flo nor Dodds managed – he scored direct from a corner! Although he claimed a total of seven scores

in twenty-three starts last season, for many fans the undoubted highlight was not even a goal. Quite simply, it was his run and cross right at the end of the Scottish Cup Final with Celtic, creating the very late opportunity for Peter Lovenkrands whose subsequent stooping header began all those unforgettable red, white and blue celebrations.

BILLY DODDS

It was not until late February 2002, in the Scottish Cup quarter-final tie with lowly Forfar at Station Park, that Billy Dodds made his first start of the season. In what was to prove to be the best of comebacks, he duly claimed a hat-trick in the subsequent 6-0 rout. Indeed, it was a case of seizing the opportunity with both feet as the (retired) Scottish international netted, firstly, with his right foot and then, secondly and thirdly, courtesy of his left. At Ibrox in early April, Dodds was again centre stage as his two goals secured maximum SPL points in the 2-0 victory over Hearts. His opener that Sunday afternoon (netting Lovenkrands' flick from close in) was followed, in the second half, by a header from Neil McCann's cross. As always, whenever he pulled on the blue of Rangers, Billy Dodds was unflagging and resolute in his tireless pursuit of success for the club.

TEAM RANGERS

CLAUDIO CANIGGIA

A legend in his own country, the Argentine international was a sensation in the 1990 World Cup Finals when he netted the winner against arch-rivals Brazil as well as scoring the goal that put out host nation Italy at the semi-final stage. He joined Rangers from Dundee in May 2001 for some £900,000 after playing twenty-five games (with eight goals) for the Tayside outfit. After scoring on his 'Light Blue' SPL debut when Aberdeen were beaten 3-0 at Pittodrie back in July 2001, Caniggia claimed another eight during the season to make him the club's third top scorer in all competitions. His 'Man of the Match' performance in the CIS Insurance Cup Final (when he 'made' one and scored two in the 4-0 triumph) was really something special, tormenting the Ayr United defence with his elusive running and clinical finishing. Indeed, a few weeks later at the same venue, the player was just as impressive in the early stages of the Scottish Cup Final with Celtic before having to leave the field injured (following a Sutton challenge) after only twenty minutes. Last summer, Caniggia was a member of Argentina's 2002 World Cup squad.

TORE ANDRE FLO

Top scorer with twenty-five goals for period 2001/02, the Norwegian striker netted a double in the first competitive game of the season (away to NK Maribor) in the very early stages of the Champions' League. Flo then hit a rich vein of form and scored in six of his next nine appearances for the club in the matches with (again) NK Maribor (3-1, 1.8.01), Dunfermline (4-1, 11.8.01), Hibernian (2-2, 18.8.01), Hearts (2-2, 8.9.01), Motherwell (3-0, 16.9.01) and Dundee United (6-1, 22.9.01). Indeed, in the aforementioned clash with Alex Smith's Tannadice outfit, the big Scandinavian (in full Flo to say the least!) claimed the first of only three 'Light Blue' hat-tricks that season on a day when Rangers were simply awesome. His final goal of last season was in the March CIS Insurance Cup Final at the National Stadium when, after a mazy left to right Caniggia run just before half-time, the striker netted his side's first of the afternoon with a low, angled shot that settled nerves when silverware was uppermost in everyone's thoughts.

SHOTA ARVELADZE

The Georgian international, making his blue debut in the Ibrox CIS Insurance cup tie with Airdrie in October 2001, hit the headlines with two goals (the first of which was executed quite sensationally) in the 3-0 victory. To say the least, it had been an impressive debut for the former Ajax striker whose initial net bound strike that night was hit with the outside of his left foot with uncanny accuracy. Four days later, in the SPL clash with Kilmarnock in Govan, Arveladze was again to the fore and claimed the opener when just nine minutes were showing on the stadium clock. Final score that Saturday was 3-1 to Rangers. Before injury took its toll late-on in Season 2001/02, the front man had hit the back of the net seventeen times (from twenty-six starts) in a total that included additional doubles in the games with Dunfermline (4-0, 17.11.01), Dundee United (3-2, 22.12.01) and Forfar (6-0, 24.2.01).

TEAM RANGERS

THE PLAYERS' PLAYER LORENZO AMORUSO

On the Sunday before last May's Scottish Cup Final, Lorenzo Amoruso was presented with the Players' Player of the Year award for Season 2001/02 at a prestigious award ceremony in Glasgow. Few would disagree that this particular accolade was no more than the Italian defender deserved after a year when, as both anchor and cornerstone of the Ibrox rearguard, he gave his all (heart and soul included!) for the Rangers cause, both home and abroad.

With six goals to his name, no other outfield player made more starts for the club last season when his total of forty-six was joint second only to Stefan Klos who led the appearance chart. Two goals, in particular, are worth recalling – firstly, a left-foot bullet strike at Pittodrie (1-0, 19.1.02) and secondly, another rifled effort that was almost as impressive in the late January 2002 Scottish Cup replay with Berwick Rangers which opened the scoring in Govan.

Signed from Fiorentina in the summer of 1997 for some £4 million, the player missed most of the following season due to serious Achilles tendon problems. As captain of Rangers, Amoruso led his side to a domestic treble in period 1998/99, becoming both the first foreign player to skipper the club to the League Championship as well as (more importantly?) the first Ibrox captain to secure the Premiership title at Celtic Park on a never-to-be-forgotten early May day in 1999.

One famous episode from last season epitomises the commitment and true worth to Rangers of the Bari born defender. When the Old Firm fought out the CIS Insurance Cup semi-final at Hampden in February 2002, the outcome was still up for grabs late-on in the game. Near the end of the ninety minutes, with the match finely balanced at 1-1, Amoruso was injured in the Celtic penalty box following a Ricksen corner. He had suffered a badly cut thigh (indeed so bad that even Celtic's Neil Lennon was frantically signalling for immediate attention to his opponent!) and most fans felt that his participation in the game was now over for the night. Of course, this would have presented manager Alex McLeish with real defensive problems as Craig Moore had already been withdrawn injured after falling awkwardly, the result of a collision with goalkeeper Stefan Klos.

To the amazement of the Ibrox legions however, the Italian bravely returned to active duty (with a heavily strapped thigh) with his only concern being that Celtic did not increase their goal tally. History shows that Bert Konterman's extra-time wonder strike then won the game for Rangers but one lingering thought still remains. If Lorenzo Amoruso had not insisted on returning to the combat zone, the probability is that Konterman would have been recalled for defensive duties and, therefore, not been in such a forward position to score the winner!

To those of a light blue persuasion, the words 'legend' and 'Amoruso' already go hand in hand.

TEAM RANGERS

THE FINAL OUTCOME
BARRY FERGUSON

Sometimes, when the most famous of victories centre on the performance of a single individual, that triumph adopts the name of the player. For example, so great was the contribution of one particular Danish superstar in the Scottish Cup Final of 1996 (when Hearts were more than broken 5-1) that, latterly, it became known as 'The Day of Brian Laudrup.' In many ways, the May 2002 defeat of Celtic at Hampden followed a similar path to glory for Barry Ferguson, with even neutral observers simply calling it 'Fergie's Final' after having witnessed the player's finest hour in a blue jersey.

Throughout Season 2001/02, there were, of course, numerous other occasions when Ferguson's star shone bright. Ask any friend of Rangers for a list of highlights and there is little doubt that the following trio would surely be offered for inclusion as part of such a package: his domination of the midfield joust with Celtic's Neil Lennon (CIS Insurance Cup semi-final tie, February 2002), his nerve of steel from the penalty spot in both the home and away games with Feyenoord (UEFA Cup Round 4, February, 2002) and his inspirational Hampden performance against Ayr United, despite those slow to heal damaged ribs, on the day that he lifted his first trophy as captain of Rangers (CIS Insurance Cup Final, March 2002).

After scoring against Ayr at the National Stadium, Ferguson netted in all his remaining games for Rangers last term when Partick Thistle (Scottish Cup semi-final, 24.3.02), Aberdeen (Scottish Premier League, 27.4.02) and, most famously, Celtic (Scottish Cup Final, 4.5.02) were opponents. His tally for the various tournaments was seven in a total of thirty-four appearances.

Right from the start of the Scottish Cup Final, Barry Ferguson was pulling the strings in midfield and beginning to stamp his dominance on the game. As early as the second minute, he made a telling contribution when his cross was headed over by Lorenzo Amoruso. Then, halfway through the first period, the midfielder's long ball into the Celtic area caused defensive mayhem prior to

Peter Lovenkrands' equaliser.
With Ferguson driving Rangers on, the 'Light
Blues' began to take control of the game even
although Celtic regained the lead in the second-half.
Then, after striking the post with a fierce drive, he turned the tables with a
magnificent, bending 'Beckham-style' free-kick which left 'keeper Douglas
without a prayer. Needless to say, Ferguson was still the dominant focal point
of his side when Lovenkrands netted the winner right at the end.

**In the days after the final, club chairman David Murray probably
summed it up best when he commented that this was the day
Barry Ferguson became a really big player, and big captain,
for Rangers. Enough said!**

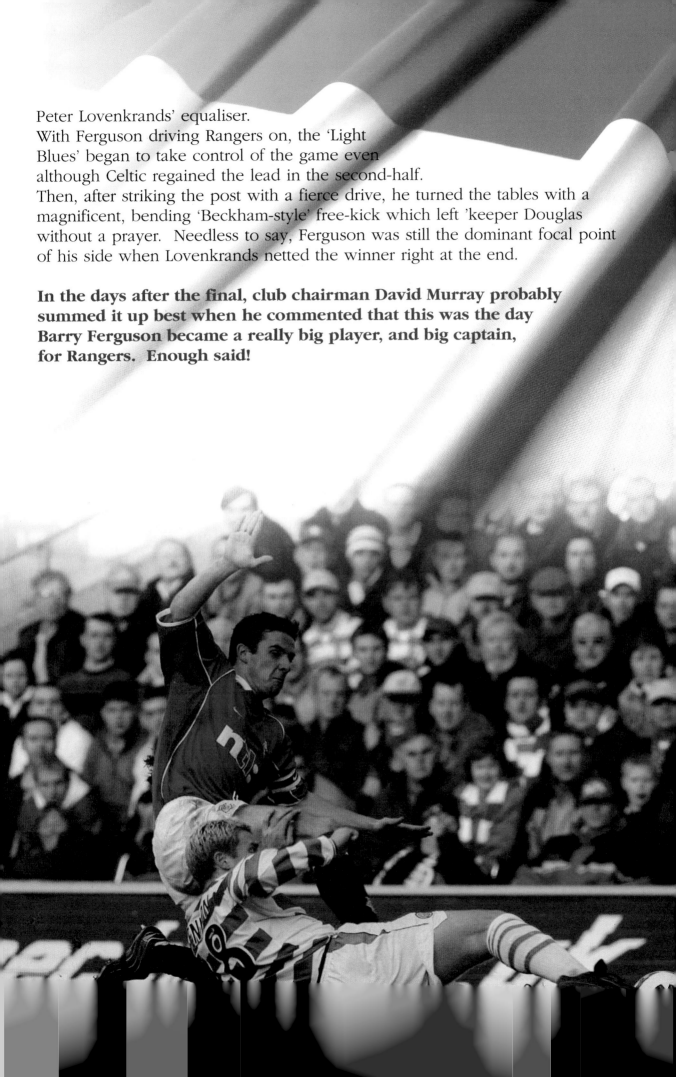

TEAM RANGERS QUIZ

1) Name the player who won his first Scotland cap in the summer 2002 tour of the Far East?

2) How many games did Christian Nerlinger start in Season 2001/02?

3) Name the three Rangers who claimed hat-tricks last season.

4) He returned to international duty for his country in February 2002 after an absence of six years. Name the legend.

5) In which close encounter game did Stephen Hughes score his only goal of last season?

6) Mikel Arteta signed from which club?

7) Who scored twice for the club on his 'Light Blue' debut in October 2001? Name the Ibrox visitors that night.

8) The Under-18 side won both their League and Cup last season. True or false?

9) Which English outfit did Craig Moore join for a short time before returning to Rangers in April 1999?

10) Who made his first appearance in blue (for Season 2001/02) late-on in February 2002?

ANSWERS ON PAGE 63

THE MURRAY YEARS

A reminder of the tremendous success achieved by Rangers during the 14 year stewardship of Chairman David Murray when the club won a total of 24 trophies.

Season 1988/89 ^ **League Championship and League Cup.**

Season 1989/90 ^ **League Championship.**

Season 1990/91 ^ **League Championship and League Cup.**

Season 1991/92 ^ **League Championship and Scottish Cup.**

Season 1992/93 ^ **League Championship, Scottish Cup and League Cup.**

Season 1993/94 ^ **League Championship and League Cup.**

Season 1994/95 ^ **League Championship.**

Season 1995/96 ^ **League Championship and Scottish Cup.**

Season 1996/97 ^ **League Championship and League Cup.**

Season 1997/98 ^ **No trophies.**

Season 1998/99 ^ **League Championship, Scottish Cup and League Cup.**

Season 1999/2000 ^ **League Championship and Scottish Cup.**

Season 2000/01 ^ **No trophies.**

Season 2001/02 ^ **Scottish Cup and League Cup.**

RANGERS
IN EUROPE QUIZ

1) Rangers' first opponents in Europe last season, NK Maribor, hail from which country?

2) Who opened the scoring when 'Gers entertained Maribor at Ibrox in early August 2001?

3) Give the date and venue when Rangers lifted the European Cup Winners' Cup.

4) This great occasion was Rangers' first European final. True or false?

5) Who scored for Rangers in the dramatic penalty shoot-out against PSG in Paris last season?

6) Name the player who had earlier missed from the spot in extra-time of the above game.

7) In the European Cup of 1978/79, Rangers met PSV Eindhoven. What was special about the game in Holland?

8) What was the aggregate score when Rangers were drawn against the mighty Real Madrid in the European Cup of Season 1963/64?

9) How many games did Rangers lose in the group stage of the 1992/93 European Cup?

10) Who received the 'Man of the Match' accolade in the European Cup Winners' Cup Final of 1972?

ANSWERS ON PAGE 63

1) **Ronald de Boer scored more goals than Peter Lovenkrands in Season 2001/02.** True or false?

2) **Rangers have won the Scottish League Championship far more times than Celtic.** True or false?

3) **Legendary striker Willie Thornton was only ever booked once in his Ibrox career.** True or false?

4) **Coach Andy Watson has played for both Hearts and Hibernian.** True or false?

5) **Rangers legends George Young and Andy Goram have the same middle name of Lewis.** True or false?

6) **Lorenzo Amoruso scored the final goal of Season 2001/02.** True or false?

7) **Ally McCoist won the European Golden Boot award in consecutive years.** True or false?

8) **During the Second World War, Rangers defeated Celtic 7-1 in the Southern League.** True or false?

9) **Paul Gascoigne joined Rangers from Italian side Lazio of Milan.** True or false?

10) **In Season 2001/02, the under-18 side won the double of League and SFA Youth Cup for the very first time in the club's history.** True or false?

RANGERS FALSE? RANGE

ANSWERS ON PAGE 63

FALSE? RANGERS TRUE?

S TRUE? RANGERS FALSE?

QUIZ ANSWERS

HEADLINE NEWS

1) Bert scores twice in the 4-1 victory over Dunfermline.
2) Rangers 6-1 demolition of Dundee United includes a Flo hat-trick.
3) Peter Lovenkrands and the Scottish Cup Final.
4) Michael Ball free-kick in game with Moscow Dynamo brings back memories of Jorg Albertz.
5) UEFA Cup penalty shoot-out win in Paris. 6) The arrival of Alex McLeish.
7) Rangers defeat Hibs 4-1 in the Scottish Cup, a competition the Edinburgh side have not won since 1902.
8) Bert's winning goal in the CIS Cup semi-final with Celtic.
9) Verdict on Celtic after Scottish Cup Final.
10) Scottish Cup Final goal-scoring hero Peter Lovenkrands.

MISSING WORD QUIZ

1) Fergie (ref. Scottish Cup Final)   2) Shota (ref. his two goals v. Airdrie in the CIS Cup)
3) Malcolm (ref. his future at Ibrox)
4) Moore (ref. his winner in the February 2-1 win over Dundee at Ibrox)
5) Ferguson (ref. his penalty goal in the 1-1 draw with Feyenoord)
6) Dodds (ref. his hat trick in the Forfar Scottish Cup game)
7) Flo (ref. his performance in the 2-0 win v. St. Johnstone)
8) Klos (ref. great goalkeeping in the CIS Cup Final) 9) McLeish (ref. CIS Cup triumph over Ayr)
10) Nerlinger (ref. his superb comeback game in the Scottish Cup semi-final)

RANGERS AND THE SCOTTISH CUP QUIZ

1) Lorenzo Amoruso and (of course) Peter Lovenkrands. 2) 1973.
3) Billy Dodds with four goals. 4) Gordon Durie in the 5-1 defeat of Hearts.
5) Seven times. 6) Nine goals!
7) False. He also scored in the 4-1 fourth-round triumph against Hibernian.
8) Neil Murray in the 2-1 defeat of Aberdeen. 9) Barry Ferguson and Lorenzo Amoruso.
10) Kai Johansen whose wonder strike beat Celtic in the 1966 replayed final.

OLD FIRM QUIZ

1) True – 49 times compared to 38 times.
2) Three - League Championship, CIS Cup and Scottish Cup.
3) 4-0 in the final of Season 1927/28. 4) After a 1-1 draw, Rangers won the replay 3-0.
5) Richard Gough. 6) Neil McCann. 7) Lorenzo Amoruso.
8) Colin Stein. 9) 122,714. 10) Who's counting?

TEAM RANGERS QUIZ

1) Maurice Ross. 2) Ten. 3) Neil McCann, Tore Andre Flo and Billy Dodds.
4) Claudio Caniggia. 5) The Ibrox 2-2 draw with Hibernian in August.
6) Barcelona after being on loan to PSG of France.
7) Shota Arveladze in the CIS Insurance Cup game with Airdrie.
8) True. 9) Crystal Palace. 10) Billy Dodds.

RANGERS IN EUROPE QUIZ

1) Slovenia. 2) Vanja Starcevic of Maribor. 3) 24 May, 1972 at the Nou Camp Stadium, Barcelona.
4) False. Rangers had reached the final in both 1961 and 1967.
5) Lorenzo Amoruso, Russell Latapy, Arthur Numan and Barry Ferguson. 6) Ronald de Boer.
7) By winning 3-2, Rangers became the first team to defeat PSV on their home patch in European competition.
8) A 7-0 loss – 0-1 at Ibrox and 0-6 in Madrid. 9) None. 10) Dave Smith.

RANGERS TRUE? RANGERS FALSE?

1) True – 8 compared to 7.   2) True – 49 times compared to 38 times.
3) False – he was never booked.   4) True.   5) True.
6) False – it was Craig Moore.   7) True – 1991/92 and 1992/93.
8) False – it was 8-1.   9) False – Lazio play in Rome.   10) True.